EVERYTHING IS
AWESOME

A SEARCH-AND-FIND
CELEBRATION OF
LEGO® HISTORY

WELCOME TO THE AMAZING WORLD OF LEGO®!

Step back through time and discover the most amazing LEGO toys ever made.

Which sets and minifigures do you recognize, and which ones are your favourites?

There are 10 things to find in each fun-packed scene.

Building a World (1932–1969)

At first, LEGO® toys were completely made of wood. Wooden animals, vehicles, buildings and more emerged from the little Danish factory. But in the late 1940s, plastic toys and bricks arrived and the LEGO Town theme began to grow.

Tractor | Wooden yo-yo | Fish rattle

Traffic police officer | Wooden bunny | Wooden duck

Stacking soldier | Red car | Brick-built clown | Wooden ladybird

4

5

The 10 things to look for are shown at the bottom of each page.

But wait, there's more! Head to the back of the book for more special things to find.

Building a World (1932–1969)

I was a Christmas gift for the Kirk Christiansen family!

Angel made by Master Builder Dagny Holm.

The LEGO Group founder Ole Kirk Kristiansen with his son and grandson.

The LEGO® Mascot was used on boxes and adverts.

This LEGO Mascot was made from LEGO bricks.
I first appeared in 1960!

Cart with wheels made from overstocks of yo-yos.

LEGOLAND

The first LEGOLAND park opened in Denmark in 1968.

I was on a ferry when I decided to make all our toys from bricks!

Godtfred Kirk Christiansen was the founder's son.

Wooden ladders were made before toys.

You're not finished yet! Try these other games and challenges ...

There's a duck in every scene. Can you spot each one?

Challenge someone to guess which minifigure from the book you are thinking of, in 20 questions or less.

How many things can you find that start with the first letter of your name?

Pick a minifigure or detail and challenge someone else to find it.

How about hunting for all the minifigures in red trousers?

What other games could you play?

Building a World (1932–1969)

At first, LEGO® toys were completely made of wood. Wooden animals, vehicles, buildings and more emerged from the little Danish factory. But in the late 1940s, plastic toys and bricks arrived and the LEGO Town theme began to grow.

Tractor

Wooden yo-yo

Fish rattle

Traffic police officer

Wooden bunny

Wooden duck

Stacking soldier

Red car

Brick-built clown

Wooden ladybird

Meet the Minifigures (1970–1985)

Minifigures arrived in 1978 and quickly became the new kids on the block. They lived busy lives in the town and enjoyed the knight life in their castles. Even outer space was a brighter place with five different colours of astronaut!

Snappy dresser

DUPLO® farmer

Ernie Elephant

Roadworks tractor

DUPLO dog

Firefighter with axe

Michael Mouse

Brick-built horse

Classic spaceman

Princess

Choose Your Side (1986–1990)

At first, townspeople, knights and space explorers ruled the LEGO® world. Then, in 1989, new minifigures arrived, with scruffy beards, eye patches and wooden legs – pirates! Adventures could now take place on land or sea, and always with a smile.

Captain Redbeard

Pirate with map

Governor Broadside

Blacktron astronaut

M:Tron astronaut

Chilling pirate

Space Police officer

Forestwoman

Futuron astronaut

Forestman

Fun in the Sun (1991–1995)

Slip on your shades and crank up the boogie box – it's a '90s beach party! Welcome to Paradisa, where you'll find pink bricks, cool surfers and happy dolphins. Look out for some updated pirates and astronauts, too.

Spyrius droid

Majisto the wizard

Space Police II officer

King Kahuna

Blacktron II commander

Music fan

Islander

Dragon Master

Skeleton

Space explorer

Epic Adventures (1996–2000)

It's time to leave the land behind and enter the Aquazone.
In the 1990s, LEGO® fans didn't just dive beneath the waves.
They also went around the world, into the supernatural realm
and even through time and space!

Pippin Reed

Dr Cyber

Willa the
Witch

Aquashark leader

Camera operator

Stingray commander

Orange Pteranodon

Robber Chief

Arctic explorer

Villainous Slyboots

New Stories (2001–2005)

In the 2000s, fans could make movies with LEGO® Studios. Will the Martians from LEGO Space take over? Can the LEGO Alpha Team stop the evil Ogel? What adventures will the BIONICLE action figures have? You're the director!

Tahu Nuva

Ogel

Cam Attaway

Skeleton commander

Tee Vee

Centauri the Martian

Harry Potter

Viking warrior

Pepper Roni

Makuta Teridax

No Limits (2006–2010)

LEGO® EXO-FORCE™ introduced the first minifigures with rock star hair! Meanwhile, LEGO Agents went on missions, LEGO Power Miners dug underground, LEGO Hero Factory protected the galaxy and LEGO Space Police were back!

Squidman

Meca One

REX-treme

Hikaru

Claw-Dette

Vezon

Spy Clops

Agent Trace

Doc

Eruptorr

Minifigure Crazy! (2010–present)

In 2010, a new LEGO® theme was out of the bag – collectable LEGO Minifigures! They're a quirky bunch from all walks of life. When they meet each other, the craziest things happen. We're looking at you, Hot Dog Man!

Hot Dog Man

Egyptian Queen

Snake Charmer

Super Wrestler

Genie

Hula Dancer

Cowboy Costume Guy

Panda Guy

Rapper

Gong and Guitar Rocker

Ninja and Friends (2011–2015)

Where will you explore today? Ninjago City for a spot of Spinjitzu with the ninja? Heartlake City for an adventure with LEGO® Friends? Underwater to LEGO Atlantis? Or into the land of Chima to meet the animal tribes? The action never stops!

Nya

Master Wu

Alien Commander

Cragger

Emily Jones

Lord Garmadon

Chase McCain

Lennox

Lord Vampyre

Squid Warrior

Lights, Camera, Action! (2014–2019)

The LEGO® universe burst onto the big screen in THE LEGO MOVIE™. Not to be outdone, Batman and the ninja of LEGO NINJAGO got their own movies, too. Then Emmet and friends saved the world for a second time. Don't forget your popcorn!

Emmet Brickowski

Sweet Mayhem

Batman

Lord Garmadon

Vitruvius Ghost

Lord Business

The Velociraptor

The Joker

Misako

Rex Dangervest

Into the Future (2016–present)

Epic adventures are built brick-by-brick and new heroes can come from anywhere. The LEGO® NEXO KNIGHTS™ protect the kingdom, while noodle delivery boy MK becomes Monkie Kid. What will you create next with your LEGO bricks?

Monkie Kid

Parker L. Jackson

Aaron Fox

Monstrox

Bag Tag
Leopard

Pigsy

Macy Halbert

Monkey King

Aira
Windwhistler

Hagrid

Building a World (1932–1969)

I was a Christmas gift for the Kirk Christiansen family!

Angel made by Master Builder Dagny Holm.

The LEGO Group founder Ole Kirk Kristiansen with his son and grandson.

The LEGO® Mascot was used on boxes and adverts.

I first appeared in 1960!

This LEGO Mascot was made from LEGO bricks.

Cart with wheels made from overstocks of yo-yos.

LEGOLAND

The first LEGOLAND park opened in Denmark in 1968.

I was on a ferry when I decided to make all our toys from bricks!

Godtfred Kirk Christiansen was the founder's son.

Wooden ladders were made before toys.

Meet the Minifigures (1970–1985)

I'm one of the first minifigures with a name!

Mary starred in a LEGO building book in 1980.

I'm Grandma!

Before minifigures, LEGO people were made of bricks.

Halt! I'm first!

The first-ever minifigure was a police officer.

LEGO Basic building sets included finger puppet figures.

I invented the minifigure.

Jens Nygaard Knudsen was a LEGO designer.

This minifigure prototype was sculpted by hand.

The first female minifigure was a doctor.

This LEGO Technic go-kart has working steering.

Choose Your Side (1986–1990)

I'm wearing the first sloped dress piece!

This Maiden appeared in LEGO Castle in 1990.

LEGO DUPLO hippos first surfaced in 1990.

I glow in the dark!

The ghost minifigure started haunting in 1990.

I designed the first LEGO Pirates sets!

Niels Milan Pedersen was a LEGO designer.

My blue visor is brand new!

A Futuron astronaut from LEGO Space in 1987.

Lady Anne Anchor was the first minifigure with lipstick.

I'm a LEGO maniac!

Zach starred in LEGO TV adverts in the '80s and '90s.

I'm Captain Redbeard's pet monkey.

Spinoza made mischief in the LEGO Pirates theme.

Fun in the Sun (1991–1995)

We're from 1993!

LEGO Technic figures had arms and legs that could bend.

You can't catch me!

Jailbreak Joe was the first prisoner minifigure.

This Alien comes from Sea-Tron, a space theme that was never released.

The flight attendant had a unique uniform.

Paradisa featured the first pink bricks – and pink mugs!

This cute, brown pony only appeared in Paradisa sets.

LEGO PRIMO figures were perfect for little hands.

Smoothie, anyone?

This chef cooked exclusively for the Sand Dollar Café set.

Epic Adventures (1996–2000)

Ann Droid had a unique translucent headpiece.

I was the player's guide in the game.

The Infomaniac featured in the LEGO Island video game.

King from the LEGO Chess computer game.

The first LEGO League competition minifigure.

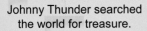

I lead LEGO Adventurers!

Johnny Thunder searched the world for treasure.

Baby Jelly Strawberry was a Little Forest Friend.

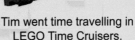

My monkey friend is called Ingo.

Tim went time travelling in LEGO Time Cruisers.

The first female police officer enlisted in 1998.

New Stories (2001–2005)

Stunt skateboarder Sky Lane from LEGO® Island.

I can't be taken apart!

LEGO Jack Stone was a new, larger-sized figure.

My name is Heart.

The Clikits™ jewellery line had just three minifigures.

It's OK. I'm an actor.

LEGO Studios unleashed horror movie sets in 2002.

BIONICLE was one of the biggest LEGO themes ever!

Christian Faber was one of the creators of BIONICLE.

Jorgen Vig Knudstorp became the boss in 2004.

RoboRiders were LEGO Technic bike-like robots.

I'm Jayko, the 'rookie' knight.

Knights got some striking light blue armour in 2004.

No Limits (2006–2010)

A secret gem is hiding in this clam!

This mermaid swam out of the 2009 advent calendar.

This statue's base said, '30 years of building to infinite skies'.

I have my own Nexus Rocket ship!

This astronaut came from the LEGO Universe video game.

Advent calendar Santa sang while he showered!

I'm very hard to find now!

Rare minifigure from the 2009 Fan Weekend event in Denmark.

Dr Inferno from LEGO Agents had unique hair.

In 2008, the Taj Mahal became the biggest ever LEGO set.

I battle a robot army!

Hitomi became the leader of LEGO EXO-FORCE.

Minifigure Crazy! (2010–present)

Happy birthday ... to me!

Cake Guy celebrated 40 years of minifigures in 2018.

The Viking Woman's helmet was a new piece.

This DJ's records referenced the names of two LEGO designers.

I have a wind-up key in my back!

Clockwork Toy Soldier was specially made for a book.

Moaning Myrtle haunted for the first time in 2020.

The track and field athlete came with a gold medal.

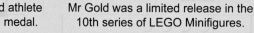

Only 5,000 of me were ever made!

Mr Gold was a limited release in the 10th series of LEGO Minifigures.

Hazmat Guy had an icky job but a unique headpiece.

Ninja and Friends (2011–2015)

P.I.X.A.L. was an android who fell in love with ninja Zane.

The astronomer had her own space telescope.

Dr Rodney Rathbone lead LEGO Monster Fighters.

Breezer was chief beaver in the land of Chima.

My eye patch is just for effect!
Ace Speedman lead the team in LEGO Atlantis.

Shh, don't tell! Lloyd was secretly the Green Ninja.

I co-founded LEGO Ninjago.

Tommy Andreasen co-created one of the most popular LEGO themes.

LEGO Mixel Burnard could blow fire from his ears!

Lights, Camera, Action! (2014–2019)

I can build a spaceship!
Benny was a Classic 1980s-era spaceman.

We have come to destroy you!
LEGO DUPLO aliens were not as scary as they sounded!

Bad Cop was also Good Cop when his head reversed.

Oh my gosh, Oh my gosh, Oh my gosh!

Batman's sidekick Robin was easily excited!

My real name is Lucy.

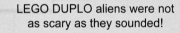
Wyldstyle was a 'tough as nails' Master Builder.

Nothing stood in the way of Nya the Water Ninja.

Honey, where are my pants?
Larry was the star of Emmet's favourite TV show.

Attractive, non-threatening teen vampire Balthazar.

Into the Future (2016–present)

There is always hope!
Wonder Woman as a mini-doll.

Niels Christiansen has led the company since 2017.

I like to dance!
Vernie, the moving, talking robot from LEGO Boost.

Man with guide dog from LEGO City.

Shields unlock app powers in LEGO NEXO KNIGHTS.

Boy in a wheelchair from a LEGOLAND set.

LEGO BrickHeadz Chinese New Year Panda.

The surprised Emotion from LEGO Education.

29

ANSWERS

Building a World

Meet the Minifigures

Choose Your Side

Fun in the Sun

Epic Adventures

New Stories

No Limits

Minifigure Crazy!

Ninja and Friends

Lights, Camera, Action!

Into the Future

LEGO, the LEGO logo, the Brick and Knob configurations, the Minifigure, DUPLO,
MINDSTORMS, NINJAGO and VIDIYO are trademarks of the LEGO Group.
©2022 The LEGO Group.

Written by Simon Beecroft
Illustrated by AMEET Studio

 Manufactured by AMEET Sp. z o.o.
under licence from the LEGO Group.

AMEET Sp. z o.o.
Nowe Sady 6, 94–102 Łódź – Poland
ameet@ameet.eu, www.ameet.eu

www.LEGO.com

All rights reserved.